I AM
The Living Christ

-

Teachings of Jesus

Edited by
Peter Mt. Shasta

Published by the
Church of the Seven Rays
Copyright 2017 by Peter Mt. Shasta

All rights reserved. No part of this book may be reproduced, stored in a retrieval system, or transmitted by any means without the written permission of the author.

www.i-am-teachings.com

ISBN: 9780998414331

Table of Contents

Table of Contents 7

Introduction 7

Hidden Teachings 10

In the Beginning 15

Birth of Jesus 15

About My Father's Business 17

Baptism and Tests 19

His Mission Begins 20

You are the Light of the World 21

Love Your Enemy 23

How to Pray 25

Let Your Vision Be Single 26

The Rich Man and Poor Man 27

Be Free of Attachment 29

Judge Not 30

Golden Rule 31

False Prophets 32

Build Your House on Rock 33

Jesus Heals Many 34

You Can't Serve Two Masters 36

Nature Obeys the Master 37

I Am Here for those Lost 37

Who is Without Sin? 38

I AM the Light of the World 40

I Was Blind, Now I See. 44

I AM the Open Door 47

Pharisees Spread False Stories 49

Who is my Family? 52

Which Seed Will Grow? 52

Good and Bad Seeds Together 53

The Kingdom of Heaven 55

A Prophet Without Honor 56

Many Guides are Blind 57

The Prodigal Son 59

As You Decree, So Shall it Be............61

To Save Life, First Lose It...................63

Jesus Transfigured 64

Have Faith 65

Become as Children 66

The Rich Man...67

The First Into Heaven 69

Should We Pay Taxes? 70

The Two Greatest Commandments..71

God is Your Father................................72

Beware False Prophets........................73

The Tribulation......................................75

Lazarus Raised 78

A Woman Anoints Jesus 82

I AM One With God.............................83

Garden of Gethsemane 86

On Trial..88

Resurrection and Ascension 91

Afterword 95
Bibliography 103
Other Books by Peter Mt. Shasta . 105

Introduction

These teachings of the one known as Jesus Christ are as vibrant and meaningful today as they were two millennia ago. He was one of the first to bring this timeless wisdom of the Far East to the peoples of the West. Long known in India and Tibet under many different names, the Church patriarchs ultimately called this spiritual wisdom Christianity. Jesus never sought to start a religion nor wanted to be worshipped, for he taught that Heaven is within everyone.

Since there are no written records of the life of Jesus by anyone who knew him, we must rely on stories passed on by word of mouth, which were written 60 to 160 years after his death and have been altered continually up to the present day. Today there are as many as 5,700 written fragments of so-called "Biblical" teachings.[1] In addition to the four official Gospels of the New Testament,

---

[1] *Can We Trust the Gospels? Investigating the Reliability of Matthew, Mark, Luke, and John*; Mark Roberts (Crossway, 2007).

none of which were actually written by the people whose names are ascribed to them, there are at least 20 other Gospels that were left out by the Church fathers in the 4th and 5th centuries.[2] In fact, many doctrines, such as that of original sin, have been added by the Church. Nowhere does Jesus say people are born sinners, a concept introduced by Saint Augustine.

The language spoken during the time of Jesus was Aramaic, yet there are no written records of Jesus in that language, and most of the Gospels were written in Greek, later translated into Latin, then into English. Most of the present versions of the Bible are adaptions of the King James Bible, which was translated into English in the 16th century by a group of 47 scholars, only one of whom understood Hebrew, the language of the ancient Jewish prophecies. These scholars turned their revised manuscript over to Francis Bacon, who further edited it before submitting it to King James. Thus, there is not one

---

[2] The *New Oxford Annotated Bible*; May & Metzger (1977)

authentic, historical version of the Bible that we can say is the official "word of God." Rather, there are many versions with varying levels of inspiration.

In editing this version, I consulted the Gnostic texts, including the *Gospel of Mary, Gospel of Thomas, Gospel of Judas,* the *Dead Sea Scrolls,* and several versions of the *King James Bible.*

I also incorporated the ancient wisdom of the Far East, which is the source of these teachings, emphasizing the Inner God Presence—which Jesus called The Father.[3] It is unlikely that any enlightened being, a messenger of God, would refer only to God's Father aspect, so when you read "God the Father" in the text, God the Mother should also be assumed.

I give here the spiritual teachings of Jesus, edited to more closely echo the wisdom of the Far East, which Jesus most likely acquired in India during the 18 years of his life missing from the *New Testament.*

---

[3] *The Dead Sea Scrolls, A New Translation,* Wise, Abegg and Cook (HarperSanFrancisco, 1996)

Hidden Teachings

Throughout the New Testament Gospels (from the Greek, meaning "good news") there are references to hidden teachings. What are these? Jesus says quite plainly that there are some things not everyone will understand, so instead of trying to explain them he frequently tells a story that everyone can appreciate on some level. To some, the story will only entertain, with a meaning that may gradually reveal itself over time, while others will perceive the intended truth immediately.

Jesus uses many forms of analogy to convey truth, his favorite being the allegory or parable, a story with an implied comparison or relationship. One of his most common metaphors is "God the Father," where the universal consciousness that pervades all creation is likened to a loving father caring for his children. In another place he uses the simile, "The Kingdom of Heaven is like a pearl of great price." Some of his most frequent metaphors are contained in "I AM" statements, such as, "I AM the good shepherd," implying that he is watching over his followers; or, "I AM the open door" (through which his sheep may pass into the pasture of the Kingdom of Heaven).

Many of his most powerful statements use the words, "I AM," such as, "I AM the way, the truth, and the life." Subsequently, later churchmen added, "No one comes to the Father but through me," changing the meaning to claim Jesus as the only son of God, and that salvation is only achieved through worship of him, rather than worship of God as the Christ Presence within—expressed by the words "I AM."

In the ancient texts and oral teachings of India, which is the source of these teachings, the Sanskrit equivalent of "I AM," invokes a deep, experiential realization of the Source. Not only does the Old Testament say that God told Moses, "My name is I AM," but Jesus knew that any statement that comes after I AM becomes a seed that will bear actual fruit. In

Sanskrit these are called bija mantras, seed essences. He knew that by repeating these seed statements, that are today called I AM Affirmations, a person becomes one with that essence. Jesus did not want people to worship him, but their own I AM, their Inner Christ; hence the name of this book, I AM the Living Christ. It is for this reason that many of the I AM statements of Jesus are highlighted in this text.

This ancient wisdom of the Far East was carried by the trade caravans from India to the Mediterranean. Anyone who has studied the world's religions will recognize that the teachings attributed exclusively to Jesus existed in India, Tibet, Iraq, and Afghanistan thousands of years before the Christian era. Jesus was a brilliant youth keen on acquiring wisdom, so even as a child he would have been familiar with these oral teachings of the East. It is also believed by many that he expanded this knowledge on his own journeys to India and Tibet during the "missing years," from age 12 to 30. The Bible says nothing about his whereabouts during this time.

When said from ego, the I AM statements may appear prideful or even blasphemous, but when they are said meditatively from the Source, they invoke God into action. This is the Presence that Jesus referred to when he quoted the 82nd Psalm (John: 10:34):

> ***You are Gods, you are all Sons and Daughters of the Most High.***

In the Beginning

In the beginning was Consciousness, and that Consciousness expressed itself as I AM. All that is—Love, Light, and Life, came forth from that I AM. That Word became flesh and dwelt among us, and we beheld his glory, the glory of a Son of God, full of grace and truth, and that Light took birth in the form of one who became known as Jesus.

From Abraham, who was born in Ur of the Chaldeans (modern Iraq) to the birth of David, the shepherd who became king, there were fourteen generations; from David to the Babylonian invasion and the captivity of the Jews in Babylon, there were fourteen generations; and from then to the birth of Jesus there were fourteen generations. Joseph, the father of Jesus, was descended in this lineage from Abraham and David.

Birth of Jesus

Joseph was engaged to marry Mary, but when he discovered she was pregnant he wanted to call off the wedding, as they had never been intimate. He wanted to find a secluded place where she could give birth to avoid embarrassment. But an Angel appeared in a dream and told him to continue with the marriage, that the child Mary was carrying was going to be a great messenger of love and wisdom. The Angel told him to name the child Jesus. Later Jesus was recognized as one anointed by God, the Messiah.[4] Unlike other children, the young Jesus sought to be alone in silence and communicate with his Higher Self, which he later called the Father. From that inner Presence he received teachings, guidance, and infinite love. He could also sense the thoughts of others, and often saw the past actions that were the cause of their present misfortunes.

It saddened him when he realized that others did not see how everything is related,

---

[4] From the Hebrew, *Mashiach,* or *Christos* in Greek, derived from *Kriste,* which is Bengali for Krishna.

and that they lived for the moment, without regard for future consequences.

He realized the impermanence of life, and the preciousness of each moment as an opportunity to learn compassion, and awaken to one's true unlimited nature.

As Jesus grew older, Mary bore Joseph four more sons and two daughters. Yet, he did not join in their games as he found their pranks crude and often hurtful. Nor did his siblings seek him out, as they found him strange. Not until after his death and his fame spread, did his brothers and sisters accept him as anyone special.

About My Father's Business

Joseph was a carpenter and taught his son the trade so that he would eventually be independent; however, Jesus knew that carpentry was not his true work. He loved to listen to the teachings of Moses, Abraham, and the prophets that had been passed on orally by the elders. He would spend long hours pondering the parables they told, trying to decipher their wisdom. His insights so surprised his teachers that they began to train him to become a Rabbi (Hebrew, for respected teacher. There was no formal ordination for Rabbis at that time).

One day, Joseph and Mary took the family to Jerusalem to attend a service at the great synagogue in preparation for the celebration of Passover. On their way home Mary realized Jesus was missing, so they returned to the temple where they found him amidst a group of Rabbis, sharing his interpretation of the ancient teachings. They were amazed at the wisdom of this teenager.

"Jesus, it's time to come home," Mary pleaded.

"Don't you know, Mother, that it's time for me to be about my Father's business? It is for this I was born—and for this that I came into the world."

"But, Jesus, Joseph is your father and his business is carpentry."

"No, mother, I am here to do the work of my Father in Heaven."

Baptism and Tests

The prophet John was baptizing people in the river Jordan, and he spoke of a messenger of God that was coming who would baptize them in the fire of the Holy Spirit.

When Jesus knew his ministry was about to begin, he went to John to be baptized. As he stood before John, the Spirit descended in the form of a dove, and many heard a voice, "This is my beloved Son in whom I am well pleased."

John anointed him with water and told the crowd this was the one for whom he had been waiting. Jesus then went into the wilderness and fasted for forty days. At the end of this time he was tested by a demon that appeared and whispered in his ear, "If you are an embodiment of God, turn the rocks into bread so that you will have something to eat."

Jesus knew how to survive on the nourishment of the Spirit, and answered, "I do not live by bread alone, but by the I AM that comes from the heart of God."

Yet, he decided that when he returned to society, he would eat the same food as others so that this seeming miracle would not distract from his message to love one another.

Then the demon took Jesus to the roof of a high temple and said, "If you are an embodiment of God, throw yourself down and the Angels will keep you from harm."

Again, Jesus knew he would be protected if need be, but he also knew it was up to him to protect himself as best he could, so he refused, saying, "It is written, 'Thou shalt not invoke God for vain things.'"

Then the demon showed Jesus all the riches of the world, saying, "If you will serve me, I will give you all this wealth and glory."

Jesus replied, "Be gone, you demon, I serve only God." He then felt great peace and was filled with the power of the Holy Spirit.

His Mission Begins

After passing these tests that tempted him to misuse his power, his Higher Self revealed his true work was beginning, the mission for which he had chosen to be reborn in the world.

He returned from the desert and as he walked along the Sea of Galilee he saw a group of fishermen. He said to them, "Leave your nets and follow me and I will make you fishers of men."

No one had ever spoken to them like that, for as he talked, they felt the Holy Spirit. His words were not empty like the priests' in the temple, but were filled with Living Truth, and they followed him.

Wherever he went, crowds gathered. He healed the sick, cast out demons, freed people of their delusions, and filled them with the realization of their basic goodness. Above all, he gave the message of Love, generating compassion in the hearts of all who heard him, and talking of the need for the universal brotherhood of humanity. Such a large crowd gathered, that he climbed part way up the side of a nearby mountain so that all could hear.

You are the Light of the World

Jesus spoke to them in parables, "You are the salt of the Earth, but if salt loses its taste, how shall its saltiness be restored? It is no longer good for anything except to throw away. The salt is the Light. If you do not maintain that Light by your attention, it will diminish and you will become as dark and lifeless as the sand under foot."

"You are the light of the world. A city set on a hill cannot be hid. Nor do people light a lamp and put it under a basket, but on a stand, and it gives light to all in the room. In the same way, let your light shine before others and they will be inspired to find the Light within themselves."

"You know that you should not commit murder and whoever does so will be put on trial; but I say to you, everyone who is angry with his brother or sister also commits a form of murder and will be judged for his thoughts."

"Whoever insults or swears at another will be judged and suffer accordingly. So, if you are going to a shrine to pray or going on retreat to meditate, and you remember someone who has a grudge against you, first go and be reconciled with that person. Only then can you sit in the presence of God with an open heart. Truly, I say you will never escape the cycle of rebirth until you have learned all your lessons and paid all your debts to others to the last penny."

"You have heard it said:

'You shall not commit adultery,' but I say to you that everyone who looks at another with lust commits adultery, and will suffer accordingly."

"You have heard it said in the old law, 'An eye for an eye and a tooth for a tooth,' but I say, you must forgive your enemies. Resisting your enemies only strengthens them and weakens you. If someone slaps you on the cheek, do not slap them back. If someone forces you to go one mile with them, go two miles. But do not let someone abuse your good will. Be wise as a serpent, but harmless as a dove. Act from wisdom, not react from anger. Observe yourself, and do not judge others."

Love Your Enemy

"You have heard it said, 'Love your neighbor and hate your enemy,' but I say to you, love your enemies and pray for those who persecute you, as that is the only way there will be peace."

"God makes the sun shine on the evil and on the good, and sends rain to fall on the just as well as on the unjust. If you love only those who love you, what is the reward? When you are in the street, and you greet only your friends, what merit do you attain? I say greet those you do not know, even those you find repulsive. Be perfect, even as your Father in Heaven is perfect, yet do not seek praise."

"If you think you are special and parade your spirituality before others, the Spirit will abandon you."

"When you give to the needy, sound no trumpet to let others know what you are doing. Do not even let your left hand know what your right hand is doing, so that your giving may be secret, without concern over reward. Your Father who sees you in secret will also reward you in secret."

"When you meditate, do not meditate in public like a hypocrite so that others will see how spiritual you are, but go to your room and shut the door and pray in secret, and your reward will be given in secret."

How to Pray

Then Jesus said, "Here is a way to pray. First, still your mind and turn your attention inward, then say to the Presence of God ,who is above you always:

O Father in Heaven,

Holy is your name, I AM,

Your Kingdom come,

Your Will be done

On Earth as it is in Heaven.

Give us this day our daily bread,

And forgive us as we forgive others.

Lead us not into temptation,

But deliver us from evil,

For Yours is the Kingdom,

and the Power,

And the Glory forever."

Let Your Vision Be Single

Jesus continued, "Do not accumulate treasures on Earth, which moth and rust destroy and which thieves may steal but store your treasure in heaven; for I say unto you, where your treasure is, there your heart will be also."

"Your eyes are the windows of your soul. If your eyes become single, your body will be full of Light. But, if your vision remains double, seeing only duality, you will remain in darkness. If there is no Light within you, how deep is that darkness!"

"You cannot serve two masters, for either you will hate one and love the other or will be devoted to the one and disobey the other. Instead, serve only the Light as your Master, and you will be filled with Light."

The Pharisees, who strictly interpreted the Law of Moses, lived mainly for the pursuit of earthly wealth. When they heard these teachings, they ridiculed Jesus, but he said to them, "You who feel such pride in yourselves, God knows your heart and finds your selfishness an abomination. The Prophets of the past preached this same eternal law, but now people distort it however they wish. Know that Heaven and Earth will pass away before this Truth changes."

The Rich Man and Poor Man

Jesus then told the parable about a rich man and poor man. "There was a rich man who was clothed in purple and fine linen and who feasted sumptuously every day. In the street by his gate lay a poor man covered with sores that were licked by dogs. He only asked for scraps of food from the rich man's table. When he died, the Angels carried him to Abraham in Heaven.[5] "Soon the rich man also died, but went to hell, where he suffered torment. He lifted up his eyes and saw Abraham far off with the poor man by his side, and called out, 'Father Abraham, have mercy on me; send that man to dip his finger in water to cool my

---

[5] Heaven and Hell may be considered different frequencies or densities where souls may go after death to continue their lessons begun on Earth.

tongue, for I suffer great thirst in these flames.'

"But Abraham said, 'Son, in your lifetime you received good things and this poor man bad things, but now he is in comfort here and you are in anguish.'

"Then the rich man in hell said, 'I beg you, Father, send him to my father's house—for I have five brothers there—and have him warn them, lest they also descend to this place of torment.'

"Abraham replied, 'Your brothers have the teachings of Moses and the Prophets; let your brothers listen to them.'

"But the suffering man said, 'No, father Abraham, if a dead person goes and warns them, they will definitely pay attention and repent their evil ways.'

"Abraham replied, 'If they do not listen to the truth of Moses and the Prophets, neither will they repent if someone visits them from the dead.' "

Be Free of Attachment

Jesus continued, "You cannot serve God and material things, but you can use material things to serve God. As you serve God, all creation supports you. Do not be anxious about the details of your life, what you are going to eat, drink or wear. Isn't life more than food and clothing? Look at the birds of the air; they neither sow nor reap nor gather food into barns, and yet your heavenly Father feeds them. Are you not as worthy of support as they?

"O you of little faith, why be anxious about what you wear? Consider the lilies of the field, how they grow. They neither toil nor spin, yet I tell you, even Solomon in all his glory was not clothed like one of these. And if God so clothes the flowers of the field, which today are alive and tomorrow wither, will he not much more clothe you?

"Therefore do not be anxious, saying, 'What shall we eat? What shall we drink? What shall we wear?' God knows what you need even before you know. Seek first the Kingdom of Heaven and God's Righteousness, and all things you need will be given to you.

"Do not be anxious about tomorrow, for tomorrow will have new worries. Allow your attention to rest in the fullness of the present. Don't divide your attention among the present, past and future, for you have enough to deal with in the present. Which of you by your worry can become happy, or add a single hour to the length of your life?"

Judge Not

Jesus continued, "Judge not, that you be not judged. Condemn not, that you be not condemned. Forgive, and you will be forgiven. Give to others, and it will be given to you. As you judge others is how you are judged. Why do you see the speck that is in your brother's eye, but do not notice the log that is in your own eye? You hypocrites, first take the log out of your own eye, and then you will see clearly enough to take the speck out of your brother's eye.

"Do not give dogs what is sacred, nor cast pearls before swine, lest they trample them and then turn and attack you. In other words, do not try to teach one who is not ready. He must ask to know the truth, and then it shall be given. He must seek, and then he shall find—knock, and the door shall be opened."

Golden Rule

Jesus continued, "Now I will give you the Golden Rule:

*Do unto others as you would
have others do unto you.*

"Enter by this narrow gate. The gate to selfishness is wide and the path easy but leads to destruction. Those who enter by this gate are many. To enter by the narrow gate of selflessness is difficult, and those who find it are few."

False Prophets

"Beware of false prophets who come to you in sheep's clothing but inwardly are ravenous wolves. You will recognize them by their fruits. Are grapes gathered from thorn bushes, or figs gathered from thistles? Every healthy tree bears good fruit, but the diseased tree bears bad fruit. Every tree that does not bear good fruit should be cut down and thrown into the fire. You will recognize these false prophets by their fruits.

"Not every would be prophet that makes predictions and says, 'God said this, or God said that,' will enter the Kingdom of Heaven, but only the one who does the will of God. On the Day of Judgment after death when everyone sees and judges their own past actions, many will come and say, 'Lord, Lord, did I not make predictions in your name?' And I will say to them, 'I know you not. Depart from me, you workers of iniquity.' "

Build Your House on Rock

"Everyone who hears the Truth and lives by it will be like the wise man who built his house on rock. The rains fell, and the floods came, and the winds blew and beat on that house but it did not fall because it had been founded on rock. Everyone who hears these words and ignores them will be like the foolish man who built his house on sand. The rains fell, and the floods came, and the winds blew and beat against that house, and it fell; and great was the fall of it."

Jesus finished teaching and the crowd stood astonished. Never had they heard anyone speak words so charged with the power of the Spirit.

Jesus Heals Many

He descended the mountain and the crowd followed. A leper came and knelt before him and begged, "Lord, heal me."

Jesus stretched out his hand and touched the leper and said the words of Power, "I AM the Presence of God healing you," and the leper was healed.

When he entered Capernaum, a Roman centurion came before him and said, "Lord, my servant is lying paralyzed at home, suffering terrible pain."

Jesus said, "I will come and heal him."

The centurion replied, "Lord, you are a holy man and I am only a soldier unworthy to have you come into my house, so just say the word and my servant will be healed. Like you, I am a man in authority over the soldiers under my command. If I say to one of my soldiers 'Do this,' he does it. So, I know you need only command the Spirit and it shall be done."

When Jesus heard this, he marveled and said to those who had followed him, "I have not found such faith in any of you who claim to be so spiritual!"

Jesus said to the Centurion, "Go, for I AM healing according to your faith," and at that moment the servant was healed.

While Jesus was talking, the ruler of that district came and knelt before him and said, "My daughter just died. I beg you, come and lay your hand on her and I know she will live again."

Jesus rose and followed the ruler, along with the disciples, and when they came to the ruler's house there was a crowd in the street and a group of mourners crying inside. He said to the mourners, "Go away, for the girl is not dead, only sleeping."

They laughed, but the disciples moved the mourners outside. Then Jesus went inside and took the girl by the hand, and said "I AM the Resurrection and the Life of this child," and she rose.

As they left the house, there was a woman in the street who had suffered from a discharge of blood for twelve years. She thought to herself, "If only I could touch his garment, I will be made well."

She came up behind Jesus and touched the hem of his robe, and he turned and said, "Take heart, my daughter, your faith has healed you," and instantly she was well. Then many began to follow Jesus. Wherever he went, he healed, cast out demons, and taught people how to contact their inner God Presence, the Heavenly Father, which could be called into action by the words, I AM.

You Can't Serve Two Masters

One of the disciples said, "Teacher, I will follow wherever you lead, but first let me go and bury my father, who just died."

Jesus said, "Follow me, and let the dead bury the dead. Life is for the living. You cannot serve two masters, both the Spirit and the flesh. Decide today whom you will serve. Your little self must die daily; then take up the cross of life and follow the God Presence that I AM, for I AM the Way, the Truth, and the Life, and what I AM you are also."

Nature Obeys the Master

He took some of his disciples out in a boat on the Sea of Galilee, and after a while a great storm arose. As the waves washed into the boat, the disciples shouted, "Save us Master, or we will drown."

Jesus replied, "Oh you of little faith, why are you afraid?"

He then rose and said to the spirit of the storm, "I AM the calming Presence of God," and so he pacified the winds and sea, and there was great calm. The disciples looked at each other and wondered, "What sort of man is this, whom even the winds and sea obey?"

I Am Here for those Lost

After the boat landed on the far shore, Jesus and the disciples began walking until they came to a table where taxes were collected. Jesus realized that one of the tax collectors named Matthew was destined to be his disciple and said to him, "Follow me."

Matthew felt the Master's love and rose and followed him. The disciples were hungry and thirsty from their travels so Jesus took them to a tavern. Inside were many people of loose morals as well as other tax collectors, many of whom cheated people and accepted bribes.

The Pharisees of the temple had disguised themselves so they could spy on Jesus, and when they saw this they said to the disciples, "Why does your teacher eat with these immoral people?"

Jesus overhead and said, "Those who are well have no need of a physician, but only the sick. I am not here for the saints, but for the sinners who are lost. I desire that my followers have only compassion and mercy, rather than pretend to be holy as do you false teachers, who strut your fake spirituality in public."

Who is Without Sin?

Early in the morning as the sun was rising, Jesus sat in front of the temple and taught those walking by who stopped to listen. The scribes and Pharisees pushed a woman in front of Jesus, saying, "This woman was caught in adultery. The Law of Moses commands us to stone such women. What do you say we should do?"

They were again trying to entrap Jesus in contradicting the ancient law so they would have a legal charge to bring against him; but Jesus rose and said to them, "Let him among you who is without sin cast the first stone at her."

When they heard this, they dropped the stones they had been carrying and went away one by one, until Jesus was left alone with the woman. He asked her, "Woman, where are your accusers now? Who condemns you?"

She looked around, and when she saw that her accusers were all gone, she said, "No one, Lord."

Then Jesus said, "Neither do I condemn you. Go, and from now on, sin no more."

He turned to his disciples and said, "In condemning this woman you condemn yourselves. You must respect women as the mother of creation, for all that exists has come forth through her. In honoring her, you honor the mother within yourselves."

I AM the Light of the World

Jesus continued to speak to those still there, and said, "I AM the Light of the world. Whoever follows the Light that I AM will not walk in darkness but will walk in the Light of God."

A Pharisee replied, "What you say is false."

Jesus answered, "Even though I speak as a human, I speak with the authority of Truth, for I know from where I came and where I am going, which you do not know. You judge according to the world; I judge no one. Only our God who sends us into the world judges."

"Where is that God?"

Jesus answered, "If you truly knew the Truth, you would also know God."

They wanted to arrest him but were powerless to move, for his time had not yet come. As he rose to depart, he said, "I am going and you will seek me in vain, for where I am going you cannot follow. I pity you, for you will die in ignorance without ever having known the Truth."

The crowd wondered if that meant he was going to kill himself.

He replied, "You are from below; I AM from above. You are of this world; I AM not of this world. Unless you find that I AM, you will die without knowing the Truth."

So they asked again, "Who are you?"

Jesus said, "I have been trying to tell you who I AM from the beginning."

Still they did not understand what he meant by saying that they were one with the Father. So Jesus said, "When you understand who I AM, then you will know that I, of myself do nothing, but it is God within that does everything. I only speak his words as I hear them. He is within me always, and I seek to do only His will."

Although they still did not understand, many trusted him. Jesus said to those who had faith, "If you trust my words then you are my disciple and will eventually know the truth, and that truth shall set you free."

They answered, "We are not slaves, so why do you say, 'You' will be free?'"

Jesus replied, "Everyone who lives in ignorance is a slave to his delusions and is bound by the effects of his selfish actions.

These actions create chains that will enslave him in the future, either in this life or the next.

"You seek to kill me because you feel threatened by the truth. You fear that you will suffer the consequences of your actions. I speak only what I have seen with my own eyes and know to be true. You speak only gossip and fake stories you have heard. If you knew God was your Father, you would love me, for I come from the Father. I came not of my own accord, but at the request of Him who sent me. Why don't you understand what I say? I tell you the Truth, but you do not believe me. Which of you convicts me?"

Someone in the crowd shouted, "There is no God; what you call God is a demon!"

Jesus answered, "You see only yourself, your own anger, and think it is coming from me. You dishonor yourself. I do not seek glory, for there is only One who deserves glory, and He will be the judge. All of you will come before that judge, some sooner than you think.

"However, if you practice the Truth you will never die, but awaken into the Life Eternal."

Some shouted, "Now we know you have a demon! Even the prophets died! Who do you make yourself out to be, promising you can overcome death?"

Jesus answered, "I do not glorify myself, but God within. You do not know Him, for if you did you would know what I say is true. If I were to say I do not know Him, I would be a liar. I do know Him, so I keep His word. Our ancestor Abraham, who knew this same Truth, is glad that I am trying to teach you now what he was unable to get you to understand in the past."

People shouted, "You are not yet fifty years old, yet you claim to have talked with Abraham?"

Jesus said, "Truly, I have, because before Abraham was I AM.

"I must do the works of him who sent me while it is still day, for the night cometh in which no man can work. As long as I AM in the world, I AM the Light of the world."

At this they picked up stones to throw at him, but Jesus vanished and they could not find him anywhere.

I Was Blind, Now I See.

Later that day his disciples found Jesus talking to a man blind from birth. They asked, "Master, was it his actions in a past life or his parent's actions that caused him to be born blind?"

Jesus answered, "It was neither. This man chose to be born blind that I might at this very moment demonstrate that I AM the Living Christ, and that as the Presence of God, I have the power to heal all affliction."

Having said this, Jesus spit in the dirt and made a paste of mud with which he anointed the man's eyes. Then he told him to wash his eyes in the pond. When the man returned, he could now see. The neighbors and all those who had known him said, "Is this not the blind man who used to sit and beg?"

Some said, "It is," while others said, "No, it is just someone who looks like him."

But the man kept saying, "I am that man."

So they said to him, "Then how can you now see?"

He answered, "The man called Jesus put mud on my eyes and then told me to wash the mud away. I did what he said and now I can see."

"Where is he?" they asked, but he did not know, for Jesus had disappeared.

Now it was the Sabbath day when Jesus healed the man and doing any work on that day was illegal. The Pharisees said again, "This man cannot be from God, for he does not keep the laws of the Sabbath."

But others said, "How can a man who is a sinner do such wonderful things?"

There was an argument in the crowd, so they asked the man who had been blind, "What do you say, since it is your eyes he opened?"

He said, "He is a Master."

"No, he is a sinner," the Pharisees said.

The man answered, "Whether he is a sinner or not, I do not know. One thing I do know is that before I was blind, and now I see."

They said to him, "What did he do to you? How did he open your eyes?"

He answered, "I told you once already; didn't you listen? Do you want to become his disciples?"

These words angered them, and they cursed him, saying, "You are his disciple, but we are disciples of Moses. We know that God spoke to Moses, but as for this man, we don't know who he is."

The man answered, "Why, this is amazing! He healed me, but you don't know who he is? Never since the world began, has anyone heard of someone healing the eyes of a man who was born blind. If this man was not from God, he could not do this."

They answered, "You sinner, do you presume to teach us?" Then they drove him away.

Later, when Jesus heard how the man had been treated, he went and found him and said, "Do you believe in the Christ?"

The man answered, "Kind sir, please tell me, who he is?"

Jesus said, "You see him before you."

"O Master," the man said, "I believe you are the Christ," and he prostrated on the ground and touched the feet of Jesus.

Jesus said, "For this I came into the world, that those who do not see, may see, and those who pretend to see may become blind."

Some Pharisees overheard this and mocked, "So, we are blind?"

Jesus answered, "If you were blind, you would not be guilty of your ignorance; but since you do see, yet pretend to be blind, you condemn yourselves to blindness—for you have turned your back on the Truth."

I AM the Open Door

Later Jesus told his disciples, "The sheep hear the voice of their shepherd, and will not follow a stranger whose voice they do not recognize."

Since they did not understand, he said, "There are many thieves and evil men around, but my sheep do not listen to them, for they know that I AM the open door. If anyone enters by me, he will be saved and will go into the pastures of the Lord. The thief comes only to steal, kill and destroy. I have come that all may have life, and have life more abundantly. I AM the good shepherd who lays down his life for his sheep. I know my own and my own know me, just as my God Self knows me and I know my God Self. I will lay down my life for my sheep. I have other sheep that are not of this fold, who I must gather also. They will hear my voice and recognize me. Then there will be one flock and one shepherd. Because I love my Father, I will lay down my life for my sheep, and then take it up again. No one takes my life from me, but I lay it down of my own accord at the request of my Father."

Again many in the crowd pleaded, "If you are the Christ, the anointed one, just tell us plainly."

Jesus answered them, "I told you, and you did not believe. The works I do are my witness, but you still do not believe. You do not believe because you are not my flock. My flock hears my voice and follows me."

Many picked up stones to throw at him, and he said, "I have shown you many good works; for which of these do you want to stone me?"

They answered him, "It is not for your works that we are going to stone you, but for blasphemy, because you claim to be one with God."

Jesus answered them, "Is it not written in the ancient Law, 'You are Gods'? If our ancestor, the prophet Abraham, told his followers they were Gods, why do you say I am blaspheming when I say, 'I AM God'? If I am not doing the works of God, then do not believe me—but I AM—so understand that I AM the Presence of God—the Living Christ."

Then they sought to arrest him, but again he disappeared from before their eyes.

Pharisees Spread False Stories

Jesus continued to heal the afflicted wherever he went, arousing the anger of the priests. They feared losing control over the people as well as loss of income if too many people began following him, so they conspired against him. They spread false stories claiming that he was the king of demons, since he could get them to leave people.

Hearing what the priests said, Jesus confronted them with a parable, "A kingdom divided against itself can not stand. If a demon casts out demons, he is divided against himself. How then will his kingdom endure? How do you priests cast out demons?"

Since the priests could not cast out demons or heal the sick, they were embarrassed. Jesus said to them, "It is not by demons that I do my work, but by the Spirit of God. This Spirit has come to you and you turn your back. If you are not with the Spirit, then you are against it. Every sin can be forgiven except those against the Spirit. If you speak against me, I forgive you; but if you speak against the Holy Spirit, that will not be forgiven in this life or in many lives to come, for that Spirit is the Light of Life."

Then he addressed the Pharisees, "You brood of vipers! You pretend to speak good words, yet you are evil. On the Day of Judgment every person must give account of every word they have spoken. The good will be proven good by their own words; but your words will condemn you."

Some of the Pharisees answered, saying, "If you want us to believe, give us some proof that you are who you say."

He answered, "This is an evil and materialistic generation that is blind to the Spirit and always seeks proof, so I will give none. On the Day of Judgment most of the people of this generation will be condemned. When an evil spirit is driven out of a person, it goes many places seeking a home, but if it finds none then it thinks, 'I will return to the person I came from,' and it brings with it seven other spirits more evil than itself. If during that evil spirit's absence, that person has not embraced the Light, he will then be worse off than before. So will it be with the evil ones of this generation."

Who is my Family?

While Jesus was still speaking to the people, his mother, brothers, and sisters, who stood outside asked to speak to him. But he replied to the man who gave him the message, "Who is my mother, and who are my brothers and sisters?"

Stretching out his hand toward his disciples, he said, "You are my mothers and fathers, brothers, and sisters! Whoever does the will of God in Heaven is my family."

Which Seed Will Grow?

Later that day Jesus went out of the house and sat by the sea. A great crowd gathered about him, so he got into a boat and moved away from the shore, and the crowd stood on the beach and listened. He taught them, saying, "A farmer went out to sow grain. As he sowed, some seeds fell along the path and the birds came and devoured them. Other seeds fell on rocks and immediately sprouted; but since they had no soil, when the sun rose, they withered away. Other seeds fell among thorns, and the thorns grew up and choked them. But other seeds fell in good soil and produced an abundant harvest of grain. So also are my words like grain. If you have ears that can hear, then you will understand."

Good and Bad Seeds Together

"Why do you speak in parables?" a disciple asked.

Jesus answered, "You understand the inner secrets, but many do not. To those who understand the truth and use it, greater understanding will be given; but from those who do not apply these teachings, even the little understanding they have will disappear. This is why I speak in parables, because not everyone is ready for the full Truth. Seeing, they do not see, and hearing, they do not hear, nor do they understand. These people's hearts have grown dull, and their ears can barely hear, and their eyes do not see. If they could at least understand with their hearts, I would heal them and lead them to the Light. Blessed are you, for your eyes see and your ears hear and your hearts are open; so you understand—and use your understanding to help others.

"This is how God works with man: A farmer sowed seeds of wheat in his field, but during the night while he was asleep his enemy came and sowed weeds among the wheat. So when the plants sprouted, weeds appeared also. The farmhands came to the house and asked, 'Master, you sowed good seed, so why are there so many weeds?'

"He said, 'An enemy must have done this.'

"So the farmhands asked, 'Then, do you want us to go and pull the weeds?'

"He said, 'No, because it is hard to tell the good sprouts from the bad, so if you try to gather the weeds you may also pull up the wheat along with them. Let both grow together until the harvest, and then gather the weeds first and burn them; then gather the wheat and take it to the barn.'

"The weeds are the evil people who grow up beside the good and cannot at first be told apart; but on the Day of Judgment when all is revealed, the weeds, who are the workers of evil, will be cast into the fiery furnace. The harvest will come at the end of the age when God will send his Angels to gather together all evildoers and send them to that fiery furnace where there will be much sorrow and wailing. Then the righteous will shine like the sun in the Kingdom of the Father. He who has ears, let him hear."

The Kingdom of Heaven

He told another parable, "The Kingdom of Heaven is like a tiny mustard seed that grows into the largest of shrubs. In other words, the Light within you cannot be seen at first and is easily lost, but as you tend and nurture that seed, it will grow and its Light will expand and fill your entire being and life.

"The Kingdom of Heaven is also like a fine, rare pearl that is so valuable that, after seeing this pearl, a wise man sold all that he had so he could buy it."

A Prophet Without Honor

After Jesus was finished speaking, he asked, "Have you understood all these things?"

"Yes," they said.

"Then I am going home for a while," he said.

When he reached his hometown, he taught in the local temple. However, his neighbors who had known him from childhood were astonished and said, "Where did he get this wisdom? Did he really do all the amazing things we hear people talking about? Isn't this the son of Joseph, the carpenter? Isn't his mother's name Mary? Don't we all know his brothers and sisters too? Where then, did he learn all this?"

The people took offense and told him to stop pretending to be someone special and that he should act like everyone else. Jesus said,

"A prophet is honored everywhere, except by his family and in his own hometown."

Because of their unbelief, he refrained from healing the sick or giving further teachings during the remainder of the time he was home

Many Guides are Blind

Later Jesus went with his disciples to the town of Gennesaret on the Sea of Galilee. The people there had heard of him and sent messengers around to the neighboring region so that all the sick might be healed, and everyone he touched was made well.

In the evening while they were eating dinner, some Pharisees from Jerusalem asked Jesus, "Why do your disciples break our tradition by not washing their hands before they eat?"

He answered them with a question, "Why do you break the commandment to honor your father and mother?"

Then he called the people to him and said, "Hear and understand; it is not what goes into your mouth that defiles you, but the words that come out of your mouth."

When the disciples told him that his comments had offended the Pharisees, he said, "Let them alone, for they are blind guides. If the blind lead the blind, both will fall into a pit."

The disciple Peter asked, "Master, please explain the parable to us."

Jesus said, "Have you been with me so long and you still you do not understand? Don't you see that whatever you put into the mouth passes into the stomach and is expelled? But what comes out of the mouth proceeds from the mind, and this defiles a person, for it is from the mind that come thoughts of anger, lust, covetousness, arrogance, and jealousy. These poisons are what defile a person. But to eat with unwashed hands does not defile anyone."

The Prodigal Son

Jesus then told the story of the man who had two sons. "The younger one begged, 'Father, give me the share of your estate that I will inherit after your death.' So, the father divided his money and gave half to the younger son. Soon this young man packed his things and traveled to a distant country where he squandered everything in reckless living. When he had spent his last cent and was destitute, he got a job with a farmer who sent him to the fields to tend his pigs. Since he was not given any food for himself, he ate the same food as the pigs. Then one day he awoke and realized, 'All my father's hired servants have more than enough food, but I perish here with hunger! I will go home to my father and say, Father, I have not only sinned against Heaven but against you. I am no longer worthy to be your son, but at least hire me as one of your servants.' So he traveled back to his home country and went to see his father. While he was still a long way off, his father saw him coming and ran and embraced him.

"Then the son said, 'Father, I have sinned, and am no longer worthy to be called your son.'

"But the father said to his servants, 'Bring my best robe, and put it on him, and put a ring on his hand, and shoes on his feet. Then kill the fattened calf and let us eat and celebrate, for this son who was dead, is now alive. He was lost and is now found.' And they began to celebrate.

"Now, the older son was working in the field and as he came near the house he heard music and dancing, and he called one of the servants and asked what was going on. The servant said, 'Your brother has come home and your father is so glad to have him back safe and sound that he is having a feast in celebration.'

"But the older son was angry and refused to go into the house. His father came out and begged him to come in and join the feast, but the older son answered, 'Father, for many years I have served you, and never disobeyed a single request, yet you have never given me so much as a goat that I might have a feast with my friends. But now, when this wasteful son of yours comes home after spending the money you gave him on wild living, gambling and loose women, you kill the fattened calf for him!'

"His father replied, 'Son, you are always with me, and all that is mine is yours, but I want to celebrate, for your brother that was dead to me is now alive; he was lost, and now is found.' "

Jesus explained this story by saying that God is the father, and the young son represents the people that have gone astray. When the wayward ones finally realize their mistakes and seek the Light, they return home to their Father. They are now more loved because of the wisdom and compassion they have gained through their suffering. They would never appreciate grace until after losing it.

As You Decree, So Shall it Be

Later Jesus and his disciples walked to the district of Caesarea Philippi, and as they rested there, he asked them, "Who do people say that I am?"

They replied, "Some say Elijah, and others Jeremiah, or one of the ancient prophets who has been reborn."

"But who do you say I am?"

"You are a Messiah, a Son of the Living God," Peter said.

"Blessed are you, Peter!" Jesus answered, "Flesh and blood has not revealed this, but the Holy Spirit. I tell you, you are the rock on which I will build my church, and hell shall not prevail against it. I will give you the Key to the Kingdom of Heaven, and whatever you decree on Earth shall be decreed in Heaven, and whatever you decree in Heaven shall be created on Earth, meaning that your thoughts, words, and energy can bring Heaven on Earth."

Then he told his disciples not to tell anyone that he was the Messiah chosen by God for this mission, for he knew that the priests were jealous and plotting against him.

To Save Life, First Lose It

Jesus began to tell his disciples that he was destined to go to Jerusalem, suffer many things from the priests and scribes, be killed, and on the third day rise again. Hearing this, Peter contradicted Jesus, saying, "That's impossible; you are a Master; nothing bad can happen to you."

Jesus turned to Peter and said, "Be quiet. That is your lower self speaking, which sets human thought above the Will of God.

If you would become a Christ, you must deny your lower self, take up your cross, and follow the Divine Presence, that I AM. Whoever wants to save himself must first surrender himself, and whoever surrenders himself will become one with the Divine Presence. What profiteth a man if he gains the whole world yet lose his soul? Only by surrendering the finite mind can you gain the awareness that is beyond space and time."

Jesus Transfigured

Six days later Jesus took Peter, James, and John with him up a high mountain. Jesus went off a little way to be still and commune with the Father. As the disciples watched, his face became radiant and his whole being was transfigured by Light. Then angelic beings appeared that the disciples realized were Moses and Elijah, who seemed to be conversing with Jesus. Overhead, a bright, circular cloud overshadowed the top of the mountain and the disciples heard a voice say, "This is my beloved Son, with whom I am well pleased. Listen well to him."

The disciples were terrified and fell to the ground to hide, but Jesus raised his hand and said, "Rise, and have no fear."

When they sat up and raised their eyes, they saw that the cloud was gone, as were Elijah and Moses, and they were alone again with the Master. Later, as they descended the mountain, Jesus said, "Tell no one what you have seen today until I have ascended."

Toward the bottom of the mountain one of the disciples asked, "Why do the scribes say you are wrong, that Elijah must come first, before the Christ?"

Jesus answered, "John the Baptist was Elijah come again, but they did not recognize him. They did to him whatever they pleased. Since they do not recognize me also, I will likewise suffer at their hands."

Have Faith

When they reached the foot of the mountain, a man came up to Jesus and knelt before him and said, "Lord, have mercy on my son; he has seizures and suffers great pain. He often falls into the fire, and also into the water. I brought him before to your disciples but they could not heal him."

Jesus called out, "What a faithless and twisted generation this is that consorts with demons! Bring the boy here."

Jesus rebuked the demon and it came out, and the boy was healed. Then the disciples were curious, and asked Jesus, "Why couldn't we cast out the demon?"

"Because you haven't yet accumulated sufficient momentum in the Light," he said. "Develop your inner connection with the Father. Then you can call forth the Light and say to this mountain, 'Move from here to there,' and it will move, for nothing is impossible."

Become as Children

As they were gathering in Galilee, Jesus talked of his coming arrest at the hands of the priests, "I am about to be delivered into the hands of men who will kill me, but I will rise from the dead on the third day."

At this news the disciples were greatly distressed, but to shut out what he said they began arguing about who was the closest to God. To settle the argument they asked Jesus.

Calling a child to him, he said, "This child is the closest to God. You must become as a child to enter the Kingdom of Heaven. Whoever receives a child in my name receives me."

Then, many people brought their children that Jesus might bless them, but the disciples tried to keep them away so as not to disturb him. Seeing what was going on, Jesus said, "Let the little children come to me, for to such innocent ones who are without sin belongs the Kingdom of Heaven."

The Rich Man

After he laid his hands on all of them, he rose to leave; but a rich young man who was attired in splendid clothes came and asked, "Master, what must I do to have eternal life?"

Jesus told him plainly, "Keep the commandments."

"Which ones?" the rich man asked.

"Don't murder; steal, lie, covet what belongs to another, or commit adultery; also, honor your father and mother, and love your neighbor as yourself."

"I obey all these commandments, Master; so, what more should I do?"

Jesus said to him, "If you truly want to enter the Kingdom of Heaven, sell all your possessions and give the money to the poor; then follow me."

When the young man heard this he went away with sorrow in his heart, for he had a great many possessions that he did not want to lose.

Jesus said to his disciples, "It is easier for a camel to go through the eye of a needle than for a person attached to riches to enter the Kingdom of God."

"Master, we have left everything to follow you," Peter said, "What can we expect in Heaven?"

Jesus replied, "When I sit on the throne in the center of my Kingdom, each of you who has applied my teachings will sit on a throne in the center of your own Kingdom, for the entrance to that Kingdom is within you.

Everyone who has let go of earthly striving and attachments for the sake of the Spirit will inherit that Kingdom and have eternal life. But many who are now first will be last, and the last shall be first."

The First Into Heaven

As the disciples did not understand this, Jesus told a parable, "God is like the owner of a vineyard who went out early in the morning to hire laborers to harvest his grapes. The laborers agreed to gather the harvest for one denarius (Roman coin that was a laborer's daily wage), and he then sent them to the vineyard. Around three o'clock he went into town where he saw men standing idle, and he said, 'I will pay you if you help me with my harvest.'

"So they went out to his vineyard. At six and nine o'clock, as the work was still not done, he hired more workers. Even at eleven o'clock, when he saw more idle workers, he hired them too. Finally, at midnight when all the grapes had been harvested, he said to his foreman, 'Call the laborers and pay them their wages, beginning with the last hired, up to the first hired this morning.' When those that he had hired last each received a denarius, the ones he had hired first, early in the morning, expected more, but they too each received the denarius they had been promised. On receiving their pay they felt exploited, and grumbled at the master of the house, saying, 'It's not fair! These last only worked one hour, and you have made them equal to us who have worked all day in the scorching heat!'

"But the master replied, 'Friends, I do you no wrong. Didn't you agree with me to work all day for a denarius? Take what belongs to you and go. I choose to give these last workers the same as I give you, for aren't I allowed to do what I want with my own money? Or, do you begrudge my generosity?'

"So, that is what I mean when I say the last will be first, and the first last in entering the Kingdom of Heaven. Don't assume you are more spiritual or more worthy of blessings than someone else just because you have been on the spiritual path longer. They may be more worthy of God's grace than you who feel so entitled and so proud of your spiritual attainment."

Should We Pay Taxes?

Since the Pharisees were continuing to plot how to entrap Jesus with his own words so they could bring him to trial as an agitator against Roman rule, they sent more secret agents to ask him incriminating questions. One of them asked, "Should we pay taxes to Caesar, or not?"

Jesus sensed their devious intent and said, "So, you want to entrap me? Show me a coin."

When they brought him a denarius, Jesus asked them, "Whose image is on the coin?"

"Caesar's image," they said.

"Then give to Caesar what is Caesar's, and to God what is God's."

When the Pharisees heard his words, they marveled at his wisdom and some of them went away.

The Two Greatest Commandments

One of the remaining Pharisees asked, "Teacher, which is the greatest of all the commandments?"

Jesus replied, "You shall love the Lord your God with all your heart and with all your soul and with all your mind. This is the greatest commandment; and the second is to love your neighbor as yourself. On these two commandments rest all my spiritual teachings."

God is Your Father

Then Jesus said to the crowd and to his disciples, "The scribes and Pharisees sit on the throne of Moses, so listen to what they say, but do not watch what they do. They preach, but do not practice what they preach. They put heavy burdens on people's shoulders, but they themselves are not willing to lift a finger. They do everything to be seen by others. They love the place of honor at feasts and the best seats in the temple. They love to be called Spiritual Teacher, but you have only One Teacher, God. You are all brothers and sisters before God. Call no man on Earth your Father, for you have only the one Father and He is in Heaven. The greatest among you shall be the lowliest. Whoever prides and exalts himself will be humbled, and whoever humbles himself, will be exalted.

"Woe to you, scribes and Pharisees, for you are hypocrites! You shut the door to the Kingdom of Heaven in people's faces. You neither enter the door yourselves nor allow others to go in. Woe unto you, for you clean the outside of your cup but leave the inside dirty with greed and self-indulgence. Start by cleaning the inside of your cup, and eventually the outside will be clean also. You are like whitewashed tombs, which outwardly appear pure, but inside are full of decaying bodies. Outwardly you appear righteous, but within you are full of hypocrisy. God sent you prophets and wise men to teach you, but you killed them."

Beware False Prophets

Jesus left the temple and was going away, but his disciples pulled him aside to show him the temple's magnificent exterior.

"You see all these stone blocks of which this temple is built?" he said. "There will not be one stone left standing upon another that will not be thrown down."

Jesus went to meditate on the Mount of Olives, but his disciples sought him out and asked, "When will these things that you talk about happen? What will be the sign of the end of the age?"

Jesus answered, saying, "See that no one leads you astray, for many will come in my name, saying, 'I am the Christ,' or 'I have a message from the Christ,' and they will lead many astray. You will hear of wars and rumors of wars, but do not be alarmed for the end is not yet. Nation will rise against nation, and kingdom against kingdom, and there will be famines and earthquakes in various places. All these are but the beginning of the birth pains. Then they will deliver you up to tribulation and put you to death, and you will be hated by all nations for your Light and Wisdom. Then many will fall away and betray one another and hate one another. Then many false prophets will arise and lead many astray. Lawlessness will increase and the love of many will grow cold. But the one who endures to the end will be saved. Then the Kingdom of Heaven will be proclaimed throughout the whole world as a testimony to all nations, and then the end will come."

The Tribulation

They asked, "When exactly will this happen?"

Jesus answered, "When you see the abomination of desolation spoken of by the prophet Daniel, standing in the holy place—this is when Jerusalem is surrounded by hostile armies—then flee to the mountains. Let the one who is on the housetop not go down to take what is in his house, and the one who is in the field not turn back to take his coat. Then there will be great tribulation such as has not been seen from the beginning of the world until now—no, nor ever will be seen again. If these days are not cut short, no human will survive. But, for the sake of the elect, these days will be cut short. Then if anyone says to you, 'Look, here is the Christ!' or 'There he is!' do not believe it. False Christs and false prophets will arise and perform great signs and wonders and give many amazing messages so as to lead people astray, if possible, even the elect.

"The Kingdom of God is not coming in ways that can be observed outwardly, where you can say, 'Look, here it is!' for the Kingdom of God is within you.

"Even though they will say, 'Look, here!' or 'Look, there!' Do not go out or follow them, for as the lightning flashes and lights up the sky from one side to the other, so will come the Son of Man in the clouds of Heaven. But first he must suffer and be rejected by this generation. Just as it was in the days of Noah, so will it be in the days ahead. Then they were eating and drinking and marrying until the day when Noah entered the ark, and the flood came and destroyed them all. It was likewise in the days of Lot—they were eating, drinking, fornicating, conducting business deals, planting and building, but on the day Lot abandoned the evil city of Sodom, fire and sulfur rained from the sky and destroyed them all—so will it be on the day of Revelation.

"Immediately after the tribulation of those days the sun will be darkened, and the moon will not give its light, and the stars will fall from heaven, and the powers of the heavens will be shaken, and all the peoples of the Earth will mourn. Then will appear in the sky the Son of Man coming in the clouds of Heaven with great power and glory. And he will send forth his Angels with a loud trumpet, and they will gather his chosen from the ends of the Earth.

"From the fig tree learn this lesson: As soon as its branch becomes tender and it puts out shoots, you know that summer is near. So also, when you see all these things, you will know the end is near, even at the very gates. Truly I tell you, this age will not pass away until all these things take place. Heaven and Earth will pass away, but the truth of my words will not pass away.

"Two men will be in the field; one will be taken and one left. Two women will be grinding grain at the mill; one will be taken and one left. Therefore wake up, for you do not know on what day the Lord is coming. But know this, that if the master of the house had known at what time of night the thief was coming, he would have stayed awake and would not have let his house be broken into. Therefore you also must be ready, for the Son of Man is coming at an hour you do not expect.

"Watch your mind lest it be weighed down by delusions, political intrigue, drunkenness and drugs, lust, and the worries of life, for the day comes suddenly like a thunderbolt for all who dwell on the face of the Earth. Watch your mind and wake up! Control your attention. Stay alert and pray that you escape all these things that are going to take place to the nations of the Earth."

Lazarus Raised

Jesus met up with Mary and Martha, the sisters of Lazarus, on the far side of the Jordan River. They were upset because the Master's old friend was seriously ill.

"Don't worry," Jesus said, "Lazarus will not die, and I will come to visit shortly," and he sent the sisters home. Two days later he finally said to the disciples, "Let's go, for our friend Lazarus has fallen asleep, and I need to waken him."

"Master, if he fell asleep, he will wake up by himself," the disciples said.

Then Jesus said plainly, "Look, Lazarus died, but I did not go there to prevent his death so that you may witness the glory of God."

When they arrived, they found that Lazarus had indeed died and been buried in a tomb. When Martha saw Jesus coming, she went out to meet him and said, "Lord, if you had been here, my brother would not have died. But, even now, I know that whatever you ask, God will give you."

Jesus said, "Your brother will rise again."

"Yes, I know," Martha said, "He will rise on the Day of Resurrection."

"I AM the Resurrection and the Life," Jesus said. "Whoever believes in me, though he die, yet shall he live. Do you believe?"

"Yes, Master, I believe that you are a Christ that has come into the world to show the way."

Martha went and called her sister. When Mary saw the Master she prostrated before him and touched his feet, saying, "Lord, if you had been here, my brother would not have died."

Jesus was so deeply moved when he saw her weeping, that he wept also. Then he asked her to take him to the tomb, which was a cave with a stone rolled over the opening.

"Take away the stone," Jesus asked.

Martha protested, "If we do that it will smell, for he has been dead for days."

"Martha, didn't I tell you that if you believe you would see the glory of God?" Jesus said.

They rolled away the stone as Jesus requested, and he lifted up his eyes to Heaven and prayed, "Father, I thank you that you have heard me. I ask now that you show these people who you are, that you are the one who sent me."

Then he shouted into the cave, "Lazarus, come forth."

To their amazement, Lazarus stumbled from the entrance, wrapped in white linen, and

Jesus told them to unbind him so he could walk. The crowd was shocked.

The spies in the crowd ran to the Pharisees and told them what they had seen. The chief priests and the Pharisees said, "What are we going to do about this? If we let him go on performing these miracles, everyone will believe in him. Then the Romans will oppress us even more and destroy us as a people."

The high priest, Caiaphas, spoke of a plan he pretended came from someone else. He said, "I wonder if it isn't better for one man to die than for our whole nation to die, and that the means we use to achieve this are justified by the end?"

He did not say this as his opinion, but more as a prophecy, implying that Jesus was meant to die to save the nation. Most of the other priests agreed and made plans to arrange his death. Knowing of their conspiracy, Jesus no longer walked openly among the crowds, but went to the wilderness region near the town of Ephraim, where he stayed with his disciples.

As the Jewish celebration of Passover was now at hand, many were traveling from the country into Jerusalem and purifying themselves for the ceremony. The chief priests and the Pharisees gave orders that if anyone knew where Jesus was, they should let them know so that they could arrest him.

A Woman Anoints Jesus

Six days before the Passover, Jesus went to Bethany, where Mary, Martha, and Lazarus, who was now in good health, gave a dinner for Jesus. After dinner and before the disciples realized what was happening, a woman took a pound of expensive spikenard ointment and anointed the feet of Jesus, wiping off the excess with her hair, and the house became filled with the sweet fragrance.[6] One of the disciples complained, "This costly ointment was brought all the way from India and could have been sold in the market for a lot of money to give to the poor."

---

[6] Spikenard (Valerian family), a highly aromatic herb that grew only in the Himalayas, a hint of the active trade between the Mediterranean and India.

Jesus answered, "Leave her alone; she has done a beautiful thing for me. The poor you will always have with you, but you will not always have me. Let her keep the rest of this ointment to anoint my body when I am buried."

When the crowd learned that Jesus was there, they came not only to see him but also to see Lazarus, the man who had been dead and was now alive. Then they believed that Jesus must truly be one anointed by God, so the priests made plans to also kill Lazarus.

I AM One With God

Jesus said, "Whoever believes in me, believes not in me but in the I AM that sent me. Whoever sees me sees Him. I have come into the world as a Light, so that whoever sees that Light will no longer be in darkness. If anyone hears my teachings and does not follow them, I do not judge, for I did not come to judge, but to enlighten. The one who rejects my teachings is judged on the Day of Judgment, that day after death when all review their past actions. What I have spoken is not on my authority, but on the authority of the God who sent me. Let not your hearts be troubled by what I say, but believe in the Light of His Presence.

"In the house of my Father are many mansions. Each mansion is a universe that contains many worlds. I go now to one of those mansions to arrange a place for you. Where I AM, you will be also."

"Where are you going, Master, and how will we know how to get there?" Philip asked.

Jesus said, "I AM the way, the truth, and the life. No one comes to the House of the Father except through that I AM. If you know that I AM, you know God and will know the way."

"Lord, we don't understand what you're talking about, so please show us the Father." Philip begged.

"Have I been with you so long, Philip, and you still do not know me? Whoever has seen me has seen the Father. How can you now say, 'Show me the Father?' Do you not see that I and the Father are One? If you do not believe this, at least believe in me and what I have done, all the healings that were the works of the Presence of God. Truly, I say to you, whoever knows the Inner God Presence can also do what I have done; and even greater works than these can you do."

Jesus told the disciples to go forth with compassion, heal the sick, awaken those sleeping in the dream of materialism, and teach those who have not found God about the Presence within their own hearts.

He gave them these instructions: "Since I gave to you freely, give to others freely. Whoever receives you, receives me, and whoever receives me receives the Spirit of the One that sent me. One who receives a prophet in his home receives a blessing, and whoever gives to you, even so much as a cup of water, will receive the same blessing as though they had given the cup to me."

When Jesus had finished, he said to his disciples, "Passover is coming; soon I will be arrested and placed on a cross to fulfill my destiny," but the disciples refused to believe this because they knew he was a Son of God, and surely God would save him. They also thought his talk about crucifixion might be yet another parable they did not understand.

Garden of Gethsemane

That night Jesus took the disciples to the Garden of Gethsemane, and said to Peter and a few others, "My soul is heavy about what is coming, but I beg you to sit here with me as company while I go aside to meditate."

Seeing the vision of the ordeal that was ahead, his heart was heavy and his mind raced. He prayed, "Father, if it is possible, may this bitter cup pass me by; nevertheless, not my will, but Thy will be done."

When he returned to his disciples, he found them asleep. He said to Peter, "Wake up! You could not stay awake with me even one hour? I know your Spirit is willing, but it seems your human will is weak."

Two more times he asked them to stay awake while he prayed, and again they fell asleep. When he returned the last time, he woke them and said, "Rise, for the hour is at hand when I am to be delivered into the hands of the workers of evil."

Even as he spoke, the priests came with soldiers, led by the disciple Judas, whom Jesus had sent to the priests so that the ancient prophecies would be fulfilled. Judas said to the soldiers, "The one I kiss is Jesus."

Judas then went up to Jesus and said, "Greetings, Master!"

Jesus replied, "Friend, do what you came to do."

So, Judas kissed him on the cheek, as Jesus had instructed, and the soldiers seized him.

One of the followers of Jesus drew his sword and struck the soldier of the high priest, but Jesus said, "Put your sword away, for all who take up the sword will die by the sword. Do you think I cannot save myself, that I cannot ask my God and he will immediately send Archangel Michael with twelve legions of Angels to protect me? But then the prophecy would not be fulfilled."

He healed the soldier who had been struck by the sword, then said to the Pharisees, "So, day after day I sat in front of the temple teaching you freely from my heart, and now you come after me with swords like a thief in the night?"

On Trial

As the soldiers led Jesus away, his disciples fled. The soldiers brought him before Caiaphas, the high priest, where the scribes and Pharisees had gathered. Before the whole council of elders known as the Sanhedrin, the chief priests asked for people to testify against Jesus so they could put him to death, but no one spoke. At last, two people who had been bribed came forward and said, "This man said, 'I am able to destroy the temple of God and rebuild it in three days.'"

The high priest said to Jesus, "How do you answer to that charge?"

Jesus remained silent. Then Caiaphas said, "I command you by the living God, tell me if you are one anointed by the Most High, a Son of God."

"So I have been saying these past three years," Jesus said.

At this Caiaphas rent his robe in anger and shouted, "Blasphemy! Blasphemy! Take him away."

Then they brought him to the Roman governor, Pilate, who asked him, "Are you the King of the Jews?"

Jesus answered, "Do you call me this, or did others tell you this is what I call myself?"

Pilate answered, "I am not a Jew. It is your own people and your own priests that have delivered you to me. What have you done? Do you claim to be a king? Answer me?"

Jesus answered, "I AM a king, but my kingdom is not of this world."

At this moment Pilate's wife shouted from the other room, "Have nothing to do with this good man; last night I dreamed about him, and suffered greatly for him."

Hearing this, Pilate went out on the balcony of the palace and said to the people, "I find no guilt in this Jesus; I return him to you."

But, the people shouted, "Crucify him!"

Pilate went back inside and asked Jesus, "Why are you really here?"

Jesus said, "I came into the world for only one reason, to bear witness to the truth. All who seek the truth listen to my words."

Pilate replied, "What is truth?"

But Jesus did not answer, for he knew his hour had come.

"So, you will not speak to me?" Pilate said, "Don't you know I have the power to release you, or have you crucified?"

Jesus answered, "You have no power over me but what my God gives you."

Pilate again sought to release him, but the crowd below the balcony cried out, "If you release this man, you are no friend of Caesar; he claims to be a king who opposes Caesar."

When Pilate heard this, he brought Jesus out to stand before the crowd, clothed in a purple robe and wearing a crown of thorns the soldiers had placed on his head. Then he said, "Behold your King!"

They cried out again, "Crucify him!"

Pilate asked them, "You want me to crucify your King?"

The chief priests answered, "We have no king but Caesar."

So, hoping to preserve peace over the people he had to govern, Pilate gave in and ordered Jesus to be crucified.

Resurrection and Ascension

Three days after the crucifixion, two men were walking to the village of Emmaus, about seven miles from Jerusalem. As they talked about all that had happened, a man came up and asked them, "What are you so excited about?"

One answered, "You must be a stranger for everyone around here knows what happened in Jerusalem a few days ago!"

"What things?" the stranger asked.

One of the men replied, "The crucifixion of Jesus of Nazareth, a prophet and great healer who taught about God but was condemned by our own priests. We hoped he was going to free Israel from the Romans, but it seems this was not his mission. This is the third day since his death. What is amazing is that some women we know were at his tomb early this morning. They could not find his body in the tomb, but they said they saw Angels nearby who told them he was still alive. So, the women came back. Some of our friends went to the tomb to check, and it was empty, just as the women had said."

As they drew near the village that was their destination, the stranger was about to continue on his way but they urged, "Stay with us, for it is toward evening and the day is over."

So, the stranger stayed with them. Later as they sat at the dinner table, the stranger took the loaf of bread and blessed it. Then he broke off a piece and handed it to each of them—and at that moment they knew it was Jesus, but he vanished. They sat looking at each other, eyes open wide in wonder. Each then told how they had felt when they had first met him on the road, how when he began talking their hearts throbbed.

Without waiting until morning, they rose from the table and walked back to Jerusalem.

There they found the remaining eleven disciples, and told them what had happened, how they had met Jesus on the road and he had disappeared after breaking the bread. As they were talking, suddenly Jesus once again stood before them.

"Peace be unto you," he said.

They were startled, but he said, "Have no fear. Why do you doubt your hearts? See my hands and feet. It is I, Jesus, the same as you always knew. Touch me and see."

As they were looking at him in shock, to put them at ease, he said, "Do you have anything to eat?"

They gave him something, and he ate it in front of them. Then he said, "Remember what I said, that everything is foreordained and will come to pass as predicted. I have done as I said, that I would die and on the third day rise from the dead. Now, behold the Glory of the Living Presence."

Then a flash of Light shot from him like a thunderbolt and at that moment each realized their own true nature as Sons of God, unlimited by time or space. They knew then the nature of the True Self, the Father, that had previously been a mystery.

"Stay here until you become stabilized in this timeless awareness," the Master said.

Then he stepped to the side of the road, raised his hands, and blessed them. As they watched, he began to dissolve into Light. He rose from the ground, ascending higher and higher until his physical form disappeared, but in the clear sky overhead there appeared a rainbow. They stood for a while, transfixed in wonder. Then, they returned to Jerusalem as Jesus had instructed, with the feeling that they were truly living in the Kingdom of Heaven on Earth.[7]

---

[7] Ascension is well known in Tibet as jalus, the attainment of the rainbow body. In this process the physical body is dissolved into the Higher Self, the Dharmakaya.

Afterword

In the light there is no darkness so it created matter to cast shadows so it could better perceive its own brilliance. The sun perceives no shadows, but the earth that is illuminated by the sun experiences light and dark, day and night, good and evil. Thus, the Source takes human existence so that it can evolve.

There have always been those who have brought truth to illuminate the darkness, such beings in ancient times being Thoth, Quetzalcoatl, Rama, Krishna, and more recently Jesus. The nature of humanity being what it is, there are always those who try to control the truth by forming organizations. Not only do these organizations distort the originally truth, but become the means to control the minds of their members. These organizations are used to control the masses. This is what the Church has done to the teachings of the one we know today as Jesus. It is not my desire to affect belief in Jesus, for a very great being responds to many who call on him by that name; I only wish to show who the man really was. Knowing the truth can only increase faith, for it will show the process by which this seeker after truth became the world teacher we now know as Jesus.

In order to control his empire, in the 4th century the Roman emperor Constantine had his court historian, Eusebius, write the official Church dogma that became the basis for the New Testament. It was written in Greek and based on thousands of documents circulating at the time about the well-known teacher, prophet and miracle worker, Apollonius of Tyana.[8]

Many people argue with this account, citing the New Testament as proof. However, as this book was written hundreds of years after the death of Jesus, and by people who never knew him, we can hardly take these gospels as historically valid documents. Then, people cite the work of Josephus, but the one paragraph that refers to a "Yeshua" has been shown by scholars

---

[8] See *Life of Apollonius of Tyana*, by Philostratus, completed circa 220-230 AD, at the request of empress Julia Domna.

to have been added later. In fact, he mentions three Yeshuas, only one of which was a rabbi, and who never did much out of the ordinary.

Josephus writes:[9]

I decided to get experience with the various sects that are among us. These are three: as we have said many times, the first, that of the Pharisees, the second that of the Sadducees, the third that of the Essenes. For I thought that in this way I would choose best, if I carefully examined them all. Therefore, submitting myself to strict training, I passed through the three groups.

On his quest he did not encounter anyone remotely resembling Jesus, or even anyone who had heard about anyone like him. Photius, Patriarch of Constantinople, writes in the 9th century:

---

[9] The following two quotations are from: www.jesusneverixisted.com

I have read the chronology of Justus of Tiberias...and being under the Jewish prejudices, as indeed he was himself also a Jew by birth, he makes not one mention of Jesus, of what happened to him, or of the wonderful works that he did.

I edited the Gospels of Jesus to help elucidate this mystery of the missing Jesus and reveal the truth about one of the most amazing beings who ever live, whose teachings transmit peace, wisdom, and universal fellowship.

The fall of Tyana lent itself to a legend. Aurelian destroyed every city that resisted him, but he spared Tyana after having a vision of the great first-century philosopher, Apollonius of Tyana, whom he respected greatly.

In a dream Apollonius implored him, stating, *Aurelian, if you desire to rule, abstain from the blood of the innocent...if you will conquer, be merciful!*[10]

---

[10] Flavius Vopiscus, *Historia Augusta* (University of Chicago, 1932).

Whatever the reason, Aurelian spared Tyana. It paid off, for many more cities submitted to him upon seeing that the Emperor would not exact revenge upon them.

John Lendering writes:

Apollonius of Tyana is said to have been a neo-Pythagorean philosopher, miracle worker, teacher and traveler. Some compare him to Jesus Christ. Others say he was the inspiration for the story of Jesus Christ. Others still say that Apollonius of Tyana was dropped in favor of Jesus Christ when the Christians decided who to believe was the true son of God....Apollonius of Tyana similarities to Jesus Christ is undeniable. They both are said to have ascended to Heaven. There are stories of both performing miracles....there are numerous letters and pieces of work by Apollonius of Tyana that exist to this day. In this way, Apollonius is more provable than Jesus Christ.[11]

Although there are no historical references to Jesus until those manufactured by Eusebius at the request of Emperor Constantine, there are references to the being named Apollonius. There were even many statues of him throughout the ancient world until most were destroyed by the early Church fathers, who did not want competition for the newly fabricated myth of Jesus.

Hidden in the name "Jesus Christ" are some very great mysteries. Why did Eusebius create this name? Jesus is the English form of the Latin "Iesus," which is derived from the Sanskrit Isa, short for Sanskrit *Ishvara*, great lord, supreme being, and the Arabic *Isa* as appears in the Quran.

---

[11] "Apollonius of Tyana: Similarities to Jesus, Historic Mysteries," by John Lendering, cited in "Apollonius of Tyana, Discovering the Secrets of Our World." Article on file at: https://www.historicmysteries.com.

Christ is the English form of the Greek word *Christos,* which is translated from the Sanskrit word *Krishna* which, according to Sanskrit scholar Ramamurti Mishra (later known as Swami Brahmananda Saraswati), is derived from *Krsh* (crush) and *na* (not). So, Krishna is that which cannot be crushed or destroyed, namely consciousness and light. In Bengali, Krishna is pronounced "Kriste," which in English is "Christ." Hence, "Jesus Christ," is a name derived from many linguistic components to invoke the concept of an immortal, divine Being.

It is well known and widely recognized that the real founder of Christianity as a world religion was Saul of Tarsus, later known as Saint Paul. He helped construct official Christianity and spread the message that Jesus was the only Son of God, without whom no salvation was possible.

The Dead Sea Scrolls show that Jesus had little to do with what passes for today's Christianity. The main conclusion that follows from these scrolls is that Christianity, as we know it today, derives from the ideology of Saint Paul, a form of imperialism in name of Jesus, a theocracy modelled on the Roman Empire, whose goal was to control humanity.[12]

I pray this book helps restore the true teachings of Jesus, whose original purpose was to free the mind from dogma and point the way to the Kingdom of Heaven within.

---

[12] "Message of the Dead Sea Scrolls: Quamran Texts," at Wilmington For Christ: www.wilmingtonfavs.com.

Bibliography

The Holy Bible, English Standard Version (Crossway, 2001)

The Holy Bible, New King James Version (Thomas Nelson, 1983)

Dead Sea Scrolls, Wise, Abegg, Cook (HarperSanFrancisco, 1996)

Gospel According to Mary (Polebridge Press, 2003)

Gospel of Thomas (Scriptural-Truth.com)

The Life and Teachings of the Historical Jesus, Lisa Morris (2009).

Apollonius of Tyana the Nazarene, Raymond W. Bernard (Fieldcrest Publishing, 1964

Antiquity Unveiled, J. M. Roberts (1894)

The Secrets of Judas, James M. Robinson (HarperColllins, 2006)

The Life of Apollonius of Tyanna, Philostratus (Translation by Conybeare, www.sacred-texts.com)

Other Books by Peter Mt. Shasta

"I AM" the Open Door

"I AM" Affirmations and the Secret of their Effective Use

Search for the Guru: Adventures of a Western Mystic, Book I

Apprentice to the Masters: Adventures of a Western Mystic, Book II

It Is What It Is, Further Adventures of a Western Mystic

My Search in Tibet for the Secret Wish-Fulfilling Jewel

Lady Master Pearl, My Teacher

Step by Step, Ascended Master Discourses.

I Am the Violet Tara, Goddess of Forgiveness and Freedom

I Am Violet Tara In Action, Lessons in Mastery

www.ingramcontent.com/pod-product-compliance
Lightning Source LLC
Chambersburg PA
CBHW020620300426
44113CB00007B/726